Belongs to .

_____

Things to remember

You don't have to be perfect

Having a bad day is okay

Small steps are also progress

Asking for help is strength

People love and appreciate you

Made in the USA
Monee, IL
22 January 2021